NARCISSISTIC ABUSE RECOVERY

A Complete Beginners Guide On How To
Recover Now From A Narcissist Abuse
And Survive Toxic Relationship

KAREN MYERS STUART

Table of Contents

Introduction

The book discusses one of the most ignored conditions, which has largely affected individuals, especially daughters worldwide.

Your mother is most likely a narcissist. We're taught to be respectful of our parents, to be grateful, and never to speak ill of them. No one ever talks about the fact that some parents are just downright evil. Toxic. Your mother is likely one of them. She's probably got a narcissistic personality disorder. Before you decide I'm wrong or that this is nothing to be bothered about, ask yourself why you got this book to begin with. Take all the time you need.

When you've got a narcissist for a parent, it can be an absolute nightmare. The worst part of this is that there are no marks left behind with this kind of abuse.

As far as the narcissistic mother is concerned, she's the perfect person and the perfect mother. As for you, the victim, you never really realize that you're getting abused since you buy into everything your mother says. She tells you everything wrong with you is your fault, and you buy it.

You'll learn how to recognize the signs in your mother and how her behavior affects you. Well, also go over what options are available to you when dealing with her and how finally knowing just what's up with your mother will affect you. In this book, we'll also cover various ways to heal from the narcissistic injury inflicted on you by your mother.

The following chapters describe the conditions of Narcissism among mothers by making it understandable and bearable. You will be guided on how to take direct action and make a substantial recovery, especially if you have experienced a narcissistic parentage.

With this book, you will learn everything you need to know about breaking free from narcissistic mothers and healing from such effects. Similarly, you will find answers to some of the questions you find hard to ask, such as "Where is daddy?" You will learn about yourself and how to interact with a narcissistic mother without ruining the mother-daughter relationship.

Finally, you will realize that treatment for narcissistic mothers is possible, accessible, and efficient. In fact, it could be your first major step in ending the narcissism legacy in your family.

CHAPTER 1:

Types of Parental Narcissism

In parents, Narcissism is a disorder that can cause harm to children. Narcissists are unable to show empathy to anyone, including their kids. But narcissists have different faces, and it may be difficult to point out which one exists in a specific family. Most times, a narcissistic mother may have numerous traits of a narcissist but may not be a complete one yet. If you are dealing with a narcissistic parent, the first thing you need to do to determine the next course of action by determining the type of narcissistic parent you have. Although it is almost impossible to change full-blown narcissists, knowing the category a parent falls in can help with the recovery process. The common types of narcissistic parents include:

The Flashy Extrovert

The extrovert mother is one of the most common kinds of narcissistic mothers you will find around. In the public's eyes, they are entirely perfect, and everyone wants to be like them. Outside, she is fun, easy to notice, and very flashy. If her child can keep up the act outside, the better the treatment meted to him or her. If the child can't, he or she will be treated with a cold shoulder.

Only those who live with her knows that she is not who she portrays herself to be. Her children will most likely have no love for her because they know she is a pretender. She gives love to only those who can help her keep up her appearances in the external world. Everyone, including strangers, loves these kinds of narcissistic mothers, except her children, which makes them desperately yearn for her love. In most cases, these mothers have a great social circle that they want to keep intact. For this reason, they force their children to do all they can to fit in by projecting what she wants through them.

The Accomplishment-Oriented Mothers

To this group of narcissistic mothers, your achievement in life is her utmost priority. She expects her children to perform their best using the standards she has put in place. Her definition of success and achievement is based on what a person does and not who they are. If you want the love of this kind of mother, your grades have to be the best; you need to be the top at every game and tournament, get admission to the leading colleges, and get a job with the most prestigious organizations.

These mothers enjoy getting attention by using the accomplishment of their kids. If you meet up to her standards, you will be showered with love and affection at every turn. However, if you fail to meet these standards and fail in the process of reaching them, it embarrasses her. Children who do this are met with her wrath and fury.

It can be very confusing dealing with this mother because when you put all of the work involved in meeting her standards, you have no support. However, the instant you can meet her expectations, you become the apple of her eye. She all smiles when she attends the award ceremonies that happen as a result of your achievements. Children with this type of narcissistic mother soon understand that if they want the attention, love, and support of their mother, they have to be at the top. This may lead the child into a high-achieving lifestyle. Besides, they are usually devastated if they fail because they know what comes next.

The Psychosomatic Mothers

This group of mothers enjoys manipulating their children, and they use aches, illnesses, and pains to do it. She uses all of these tools to ensure attention stays on her at all times. She needs to prioritize others, and any child who wants the love and attention of this mother has to play the role of a caretaker. If you call her out on her behavior or fail to fall for her antics, she gets into a health crisis. This usually works in making you feel guilty for failing to be there when your mother needed you the most.

The only important thing to a mother is for her child to be at her beck, caring for her. This strategy is also useful for the mother in getting away from difficult situations. If she hears something terrible that she doesn't want to deal with, feigning a particular illness is her next option. If you heard this phrase; "Don't break the news to your mother, or her sickness will worsen," then you may have been dealing with a psychosomatic mother.

In addition to caring for her, another way to get attention from this mother is to fall sick too. This is something many children find out later on. The reason for this is that being sick makes them to connect on mutual ground.

However, if the child's sickness is worse than that of the mother and ends up taking up all of the attention, the mother will not be pleased with it. She feels entitled to all the care and won't be happy when her child takes it all.

The Addicted Narcissistic Mother

These narcissistic mothers deal with substance abuse. However, their behavior is more prominent whenever they are under the influence of any substance they are addicted to. Anytime the effect of the substance wears off, they portray fewer narcissistic behaviors. But sometimes, this is not the case. To these mothers, they prioritize the substance. Nobody else matters until they satisfy their addiction. They must cater to their addiction before they do anything else.

The Subtly Abusive

These mothers share some similarities with extrovert mothers. They are very particular about how those on the outside see them and would prefer if no one outside was aware of her abuses at home. These mothers usually have a personality they display in private and a different one in public.

On the outside, they are the kindest, sweetest, loving, and most sensitive mother, any child, can have. However, when they are home, they become mean and abusive. For children who live with these types of mothers, their lives can be confusing.

Also, this mother can say one thing in public and say something entirely different in private. For instance, when in public, she could announce to everyone how proud she is of her child in a room. But in private, she will continuously tell her child how much of a disappointment they are. This kind of inconsistent behavior can be very confusing for the child and can lead to a long-term ripple effect.

The Emotionally Needy

Most narcissistic mothers have this trait. However, those mothers in this category make it more prominent than others. They dump all of their emotional baggage on their children and expect them to listen, care for, and understand them. In an ideal family, this is supposed to be the other way around.

In time, the children begin to play the roles of therapists trying to solve problems they should not have any business solving in the first place. While this is going on, the children's emotional needs are ignored, and even when they do garner the courage to ask their mother for help, the help they get from her is almost insignificant.

The Flamboyant Extroverted Mother

This one is the ideal mother for everyone out there. She is loved by everyone, neighbors, friends, and even random strangers because she is very nice and friendly.

She has it all going in the public eye, and she constantly strives to maintain that image. She will be totally offended by anyone or anything that might seem to change this perception.

However, she secretly is a monster in her home to the children. She will control them and be mean to them but still ensuring that whatever they do in the public eye always makes her look like the best mother in the world. The children fear her and cannot seek help as they feel like there is no way out, and no one would believe them anyway.

The Addict

Substance abuse always ends up turning people into something they should not be. Mothers who abuse drugs or are alcoholics always tend to end up being narcissistic as the addiction gets to control their emotions and everything they do. They also always choose substance over family; hence any time a misunderstanding comes up, and they will run to the bottle and blame it later. They do not take responsibility for anything, and when cornered, they will always abuse. Most of them, when high due to addiction, tend to vent all the anger and pain on the children.

A few times, they are good mothers when they are sober, but it only lasts for a short while. They will also get high and constantly blame their children for the addiction.

The Mean Mother

This one is mean to her children and will not want her children to have what she cannot have or never had. She will constantly interfere in the good things that the children might have, so she can always be the one looking good or being praised. She will not let the daughter have a good car if she doesn't have one.

She will not let the son have a nice house if she has not built one for her. This limits her children so much, as they cannot make any progress in life that is better than hers.

The children end up doing things in secret so they can enjoy some luxuries without her knowledge.

The Success-Oriented Mother

This one is only concerned about what the children accomplish and nothing else. She will constantly compare her children with their peers if they do look like they have more accomplishments than her children. She is constantly happy when her children get luxurious things, especially if she knows she can benefit from them. She is happy to visit her children in big homes, be driven around in big cars, and boast of how successful her family is. Anyone that is not successful in her family will constantly be intimidated and ignored as she will constantly make it clear that she does not associate with failures. These kinds of mothers push their children too hard that they cannot think of anything else except the next best car, phone, etc.

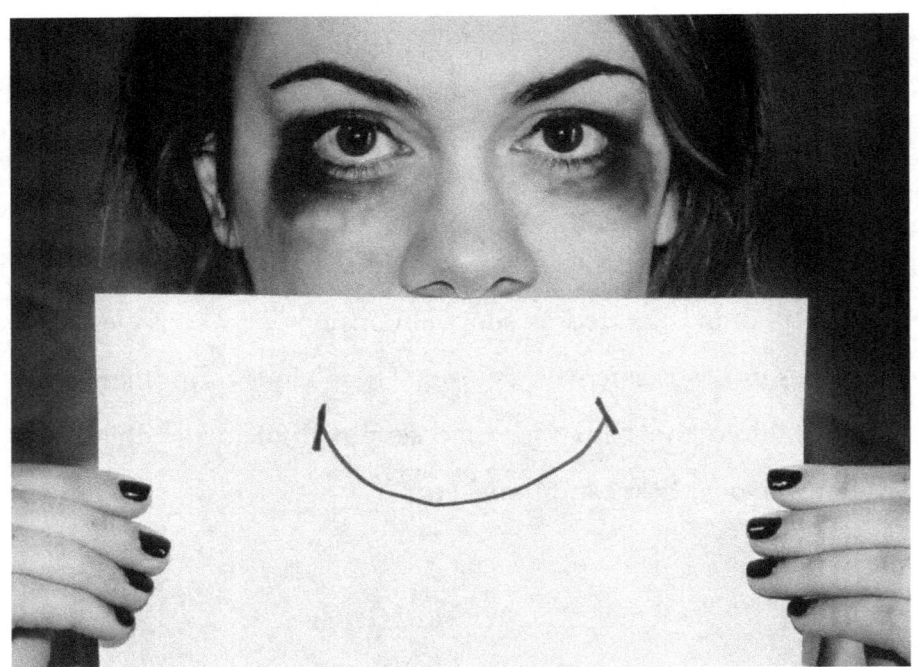

CHAPTER 2:

Recognizing a Narcissistic Parent

The narcissist is the perfect pretender. She is a wolf in sheep's clothing. The narcissist understands that her true self is unacceptable. Because of this, she does her best to create a false persona. The narcissist is the ultimate method actor—with the ability to completely abandon one character or mask in favor of another in a heartbeat. Why is this so? Remember, the narcissist is a predator. The last thing a predator need is for its prey to recognize it when it crouches, ready to kill.

The Narcissist's Vibe

Narcissists are both similar to and different from each other. They are pretty much the same thing at their core and have the same desire—being the center of attention and dominating everything and everyone. They all do this by merely manipulating others into giving them the reactions they want. However, this is where the similarities end. All narcissists live in different situations, and so they adapt accordingly.

Malignant narcissists are arrogant. They are vain, cocky, entitled, and they brag a lot. They are also utterly grandiose, and it's hard to miss their arrogance in the way they carry themselves, the way they dress, the way they talk.

Not all narcissists are this way, though; some narcissists are skilled at keeping all that haughtiness tightly sealed and under wraps, cloaked with faux modesty. They only ever let their freak flag fly when they're with those who are close to them.

Narcissists are adept at adapting to their surroundings. If a narcissist would ordinarily be flamboyant, gregarious, and loud in the city, he would tone it down in the smaller towns where such behavior is frowned upon. The narcissist knows when it's time to be all grandiose—when it matters that they pass themselves off as important—and when it's time to be "humble"—so everyone marvels at how remarkably modest he is.

It might seem that because the narcissist is so adaptable, it would be hard to detect her. But you can. All you need to do is look a little bit closer. Grandiosity is not an easy thing to hide, no matter how subtle the narcissist is about it. You can detect it in the way they relate with others. There's a hint of judgment in the way they talk with others. It's there in the presumptions they have about what they feel ought to be done, as they present their opinions as mere suggestions, and touched up with that false modesty and humility. Then there's the bragging. It always creeps in somehow.

Not all narcissists are elegantly dressed, have a house in the Hamptons, a movie in the works, and act out when their trailer is not set just so. Some narcissists present themselves as regular people. They dress simply. They don't seem the least bit vain and don't say too much.

Then others talk a lot—and you'll usually find these types working as preachers or politicians. A few others are dictators, greatly feared. The point to take away from all this is that you can't assume just because someone "fits the profile"—whatever that profile is in your head—they are a narcissist.

The Image Is Everything

The narcissist does not mess about when it comes to her image. She adapts to whatever the situation or environment requires of her. When she needs attention, she knows just how to be and what to wear to stand out. When it's time to get approval for something, she knows the perfect way to blend right in with the crowd.

The narcissist is not two-faced. She has many faces. She's different when she's at home and different when she's at work. She's different when she's with her colleagues and different when she's with her family. She's one way when you're dating her, and she's another way entirely when you're married. It's almost as if a narcissist has multiple personas. You can never be quite sure of anything when it comes to the narcissist. You can bank on one thing, though—his image is the complete opposite of who he really is.

Astute Observers

The narcissist pays special attention to the way humans behave, both as individuals and in group settings. They understand the dynamics of human interaction better than the average person. It's natural for human beings to figure out how to gain approval and acceptance and then adopt that behavior. The narcissist knows this.

How she takes advantage of this tendency in humans is by being mercurial. She blows hot, then cold, then not at all. These arbitrary and random behavior keeps the people around her in a state of suspense, uncertainty, and insecurity. The people around her become afraid of saying or doing anything for fear that it might be the wrong thing. And when you're around her, no matter what you say or do, it's never right.

As far as the narcissist is concerned, they alone deserve all the attention. If they can't get it for themselves, then there will be trouble. Usually, a narcissist will not get that much attention at home. That's because everyone at home already knows them for who they are. What does the narcissist do then? He must seek some attention somewhere by either being aggressive and causing fights, running his mouth, or generally being a nuisance.

Control Tactics of Narcissistic Mothers

The narcissistic mother uses various control tactics to make you do what she wants without a lot of questions.

Mind control is a method where the mother uses many manipulative tactics to affect your behaviors and brain function.

Here are a few methods that the narcissistic mother ill-use frequently to get to you:

Bandwagon Effect

The narcissistic mother will try and make you go along with other things just because other people are doing it. They understand the power of numbers and will follow others to get the right attention. For instance, they will desire many followers on social media to get their thrill on. They often make use of group thinking to play on the fears of other people.

They will make it seem that other people agree with her to make you do something for her. If other people are buying a particular item, she will tell you how "everyone has it" so that she can persuade you into picking up the item.

Only Two Options

The narcissistic mother will give you only two options—either you do this or…

They view the world in just two options that you have to choose from, they will get their comfort from the two choices, and they will force you to choose from the two so that they have some power over you.

False Flattery

They will butter you up so that you will be more receptive to their needs when they ask for anything. They will pile you with compliments that don't make sense only to get what they want, and then they show their true colors.

They will try their best to get what they want and then will leave once they get what they want.

Incredulity

They act as if what you have done is very unbelievable. They usually use the tactic when they don't get what the other person is saying. Rather than admit that they don't get what you are saying, they will pretend that what you are saying or doing is beyond belief at all times.

This is usually common when you have a valid concern, yet the other person wishes to rubbish them. The narcissistic mother will take up a stance that will make you feel like you are telling a lie.

They Label You

The narcissistic mother will apply negative labels to their kids. These labels are single words that will humiliate you and make you feel as if you are worthless. They will use phrases such as "needy," "losers," and many more. The aim is to make you feel like the description of the phrase.

CHAPTER 3:

What Is the Difference Between Narcissistic Mothers and Narcissistic Fathers?

I deally, when a child cannot get support from the mother, the next logical person to run to is the father. A father is the family protector and should typically safeguard his children from abuse.

However, in the home run by narcissistic mothers, things are a bit different. The father is usually the enabler, as any strong man with his self-esteem intact won't stand for all of the abuse. In fact, he probably would have left the toxic relationship a long while back.

But a man with properly set boundaries who has respect for himself would never have settled for a toxic woman like the narcissist in the first place. Even if he unluckily ended up with one due to all manipulation strategies, the relationship would have ended quickly.

This is why narcissists go after those they believe they can bully and condition to behave the way they desire. The men who settle for narcissistic women may have dealt with some form of abuse growing up.

Narcissistic parents themselves may have also raised them. They could have been golden sons searching for a woman to treat them like their mother did. They could also have been the scapegoat son, trying to get a woman similar to their mother to offer them the love their mothers never gave.

A man who wants to settle for a narcissistic wife must be able to do all she desires. He must worship her very existence and continue to let her know how flawless she is always. He must give her own desires priority over his own to ensure she is pleased with all times.

How Do Narcissist Mothers Keep Their Spouses in Check?

Narcissistic wives have complete control of their husbands. Similar to how they manipulate their children, narcissistic mothers do the same to their spouses too.

They can use love and sex as weapons to keep their spouses in check. They continuously keep them confused and may use gaslighting to get them to doubt everything they know.

In the end, these husbands begin to believe the truths they are conditioned to believe by their spouses. The narcissistic wife tells them what is wrong and what is right. They also learn what they are supposed to do and what they are not allowed to do.

CHAPTER 4:

Possible Impacts of a Narcissistic Parent on Our Lives

The impact that narcissistic parents can have on their children is extreme. It can affect the psychological development of the child. This will play a role in their behaviors. Also, their attitude, emotions, and sense of ethics may be thrown off. The child of a narcissistic parent will have unrealistic expectations that they are trying to meet. This is almost impossible and can completely change how a child deals with the world.

It is important to understand that pleasing a narcissistic parent is almost impossible. As a child, this will often lead to them feeling like they are not seen or heard. Their reality will be warped. Children that have narcissistic parents are treated as property rather than a person. This is going to have significant effects on them as they grow and develop.

With these toxic parenting skills, many children raised in these households are not valued as people. Instead, they are praised or criticized based solely on what they are doing. They don't learn how to understand their feelings, and this can lead to terrible self-doubt. As the child of this situation grows up, this self-doubt will play a significant role in their relationships.

When you are in a situation where you are rated on how you look or how intelligent you are, you most likely won't understand or put importance into how you are feeling. It is a vicious cycle that can, unfortunately, turn the child of a narcissistic parent into a narcissist. Being real is not something that will be taught to the child dealing with these types of parents. They will believe that their image is exceptionally more important than their true selves.

Keeping secrets is a big part of the narcissist's ways. In turn, the child will keep secrets that will keep their family or parent well protected. They will not find themselves, as they will be intertwined with what the narcissistic parent wants. There will not be nurturing, and, typically, these children will feel emotionally barren. When a child feels this way, it is tough for them to trust other people. This is because they understand that they're being manipulated and used by those that are supposed to love them the most.

As parents, we are supposed to be there for our children However, the opposite happens with narcissistic parents. This stunts the development of a child in a variety of different ways Where they should feel loved and accepted for who they are, they will instead feel as if they're being judged and criticized at every corner. This can lead to some major frustration for the child. They will continuously seek approval and love but will likely never be able to find it. Not from their parents, at least.

When you are raised in a home where nothing you ever do is good enough, it will impact the rest of your life unless you do some work to correct the damage that has been done. Without a role model for good connections with other people, it is tough to develop these skills. They won't understand what healthy boundaries in a relationship look like. Often, children who grow up in these types of situations become exceptionally codependent. They don't understand nor learn how to take care of themselves emotionally, physically, or mentally.

CHAPTER 5:

Narcissistic Mother

The way Narcissism manifests in mothers is explicitly unique, as children see their parents in a way that no one else does. Even a healthy parent-child relationship is likely to be a unique experience to them. Mothers tend to be more comfortable around their children, meaning that they can open up and express their true selves better around their children.

This is generally shown in a gentler and softer, nurturing manner for mothers who do not have Narcissism. However, for those mothers who do have Narcissism, this is usually a relationship where the Narcissism will play out in a far more offensive and overwhelming manner than it would in any other relationship. In other words, narcissistic mothers tend to abuse their children, especially their daughters, more than anyone else.

Understanding how Narcissism manifests in mothers is the best way to identify where your mother is abnormal compared to other mothers and how these abnormalities are linked to her narcissistic personality disorder.

A narcissist parent uses their position of authority to keep their children in check in unhealthy manners. If you notice any of the traits we will be discussing below in your parent, you may be dealing with a narcissistic parent.

She Projects Her Desires Through You

Narcissists only can care for themselves and no one else. This is the case even with narcissistic parents.

They tend to live through the lives of their children in really unhealthy ways. For instance, if a parent had experiences she desired when she was younger but could not achieve, she may try to live it through her kids.

To achieve this, she may try to force her kids to participate in activities that they have no interest in re-experiencing her past days. So, if your mother continues to force you to take dance classes or music classes even though what you want is to take part in a poetry class, then you may be dealing with a narcissistic parent.

However, you need to understand that many mothers urge their kids to participate in supplementary activities at some point. If this happens, this may not mean you are the child of a narcissistic parent. But if your mother says things like, "I always wanted to learn music but never had the chance, so you should be glad you can," before going ahead and forcing you to take music classes, then this could be a clear sign.

She Is Never Wrong

As humans, it is normal to have disagreements and arguments. During these arguments, you will learn that sometimes you were wrong, and other times you were right. No one is always right, and this is the same case for everyone. However, narcissists believe they are always right and never at fault. This is the case, especially when it involves a narcissistic mother. She makes herself the victim anytime there is an argument, even when the argument does not concern her. During arguments, instead of accepting her faults and making amends, she becomes defensive and may even try to guilt-trip you. If you are familiar with any of these, then you may have a narcissistic mother on your hands.

Your Needs Do Not Matter

Narcissists give themselves priority above anyone else. Narcissistic parents often ignore their kids and pay attention to their own needs above. As opposed to caring for her children, Narcissistic mothers may focus on their hobbies, career, and other things she believes are more important.

Due to this, children of narcissistic parents often learn to fend for themselves at an early age. If the majority of your childhood was spent with family members, nannies, by yourself, or with other guardians, then you may have had a narcissistic mother.

However, do not be too quick to judge. A busy mother may just be trying to get the best life for her kids. This alone can't be used to determine she is a narcissistic parent.

It Is Easy to Offend Her

Narcissists always crave attention. In fact, they thrive on this attention and would do all they can to get it. Parents in this category look for any reason to be offended, especially when they feel criticized. Even the most straightforward and irrelevant things can get a narcissistic parent offended. Sometimes, giving compliments to others may not go well with them. For example, if you tell your mother her friend dresses nice, and she snaps back suddenly with, "Well, I dress nice too, don't I?"

If all of these are familiar scenarios, then you may be dealing with a narcissistic mother.

She Places All Her Emotional Burden on You

This is very common in homes with single parents. Under normal circumstances, having a proper communication line between parents and kids is not bad, but when you have started to play the role of a therapist to your mother, it is a huge problem.

Ideally, parents should be responsible for meeting the emotional needs of their kids. They are the ones children should be able to run to when there is a problem and get help. However, when the roles become reversed and stay this way, then this could be a sign of trouble.

As the narcissistic parent continues to depend on their kids emotionally, it may result in unhealthy codependency between both parents and kids. This is usually in addition to the kids fending for their every need. And in the rare situation that the kids complain, the mother may guilt-trip them into making them feel they are unfair by refusing to meet her every need.

If you have ever found yourself in this situation, it is a compelling indication of a narcissistic mother.

She Will Deny Everything

Part of Narcissistic Personality Disorder is placing blame on other people and denying wrongdoing. The biggest reason a narcissist will react this way is that they have a strong need to uphold their best image. Even if people realize they are lying or denying involvement, a narcissist will continue to do whatever necessary to act like they did nothing wrong.

As a child, you were often blamed for what your mother did. This is because you were the easiest target to use since you were less likely to argue or speak the truth to avoid receiving her wrath. Furthermore, most children want to protect their parents, just as their parents are supposed to protect them. Even if you didn't receive protection from your mother, you still felt the urge to protect her.

Your Mother Lies to You

Narcissists are known to lie. They do this in order to manipulate or control you to get what they want. They will also lie to themselves. They need to do this in order to make themselves look better in front of other people.

Many narcissists are believed to be compulsive liars, but this isn't necessarily true. Narcissists usually know when they are lying, whereas compulsive liars don't always understand they are lying.

It is important to remember that everyone lies at some point in their lives. We also lie for different reasons. While you were often hurt by your mother's lies, it is important to understand this is another part of Narcissism.

They lie to cover their tracks and avoid looking bad to someone else. They may also lie to try to feel better about themselves. This is especially true for a narcissist who understands their mental disorder and is trying to overcome it.

She Is Manipulative

One of the biggest traits about a narcissist is they are manipulative. A narcissist will use various manipulation tactics to gain control of the situation. For example, your mother negatively compares you to one of your siblings, shames or embarrasses you when you don't comply with what she wants, or says you are ungrateful and don't care about her.

There are various forms of manipulation, ranging from good to bad. A narcissist will rarely use a good form of manipulation, such as using manipulation to help someone else, hence having an altruistic purpose.

For example, when a therapist manipulates you by asking a question in a certain manner, they help you understand yourself better. Negative forms of manipulation are used when someone tries to get you to do something for their own benefit. These are the forms of manipulation your mother will use.

She Diverts All Conversations to Herself

By now, you should understand that attention is something narcissists can't do without. Narcissistic parents like to make every conversation about them.

For instance, if you have a conversation about something important that happened to you, narcissistic mothers always find a way to make it about them. Rather than listening to you, they ignore what you are saying and instead make it about them.

If you find that every conversation you have with your mother is always diverted to her interest, then you may be dealing with a narcissist.

She Is Extremely Competitive

In healthy relationships between parents and kids, the parents may sometimes allow their kids to beat them at games. These could be when playing board games, video games, or races. The reason for doing this is to encourage a healthy spirit of competition. It also helps build confidence in kids. This is also the case with a few animals that let the younger ones win.

However, when it involves narcissistic parents, this is not the case. They hardly allow their kids to win anything, and this goes past games and spreads into real life. A narcissistic mother may continuously feel the need to feel more beautiful and better dressed than her daughter.

She doesn't care about how she achieves this, even if she has to go through some plastic surgery. Sometimes she may even flirt around during gatherings to ensure attention does not deviate from her. Competition can also come in other areas like finance, sports, and so on.

She Puts You Down

In a bid to make herself feel better than others, she continuously puts you and everyone around her down. This is a common trait among narcissists, and narcissistic mothers are not different.

They don't hesitate to put down their children and always remind them how much better they are than them. In most situations, they do not even give them any form of compliment whatsoever.

A narcissistic mother will leverage insults, criticism, and manipulation to reduce the confidence of their kids. Sometimes, she may downplay their achievements even though her children have done well.

The only time your achievements are acknowledged is when she can take full credit for them.

They Use Love and Affection as Weapons

Narcissistic mothers understand how important love and affection are to their kids, and they use it to their advantage.

As a form of reward, they show love and affection to their kids when they do things they want. And when they do show this love, they ensure it is in the full glare of the public, so they are deemed good parents.

However, they also take back this love and affection as punishment when their kids fail to do something they desire.

She Does Not Respect Boundaries

Narcissistic mothers don't respect the boundaries of their kids. They may take up their time and even the properties of their kids without permission. There is no privacy in your bedroom either, as she can waltz in at any moment without warning.

When this happens, the only reason you get is that it is her home, and she can do whatever she wants. Even as an adult, she may barge into your home without notice or regard for your privacy.

She asks a lot of intrusive questions and goes through your diary, texts, and emails without your permission. She does this to determine your feelings to use them against you. Even things as simple as choosing your clothes can be a pain as she wants to control every aspect of your life, including your style choices. If you live with a mother who undermines every one of your boundaries, then she might be a narcissist.

A Mother That Is Threatened by Her Child

Narcissistic mothers often experience the feeling of being threatened by their children in the sense that they worry that their children are likely to take attention and admiration away from themselves. When narcissistic mothers notice their children are getting attention around any given subject, such as excelling in school, they will often begin to feel threatened. They will attempt to minimize the value of the child's achievements.

A significant way they do this is through how they talk to others, using sayings like:

- "Finally, you're good at something for once!"

- "It's about time you bring home an award for something."

- "Wait, you mean you did something good? Wow."

Speaking in a way that makes it seem like the child is otherwise terrible is a way that a narcissistic mother can control the amount of attention the child receives. They may receive care around this one thing, but through her words, she tarnishes the child's reputation and therefore prevents the child from receiving further accolades anywhere else in their lives.

This way, she can earn those accolades for herself and gain all of the excessive attention and admiration she needs from others.

An Effort at Self-Fulfillment Through You

Another big way that narcissistic mothers can be identified through their symptoms is through attempting to inflate their sense of self through you.

Narcissistic mothers frequently live through their children or use their children as a way to inflate their sense of self further. They generally do this because they know that children cannot identify what is going on at young ages, and therefore they cannot stop the abuse from happening.

By the time they are old enough to speak up, the mother has either made them too afraid to try or has already groomed everyone else to believe that the child is a problematic liar so that no one thinks the child.

In the end, the child is forced to live in a mental prison that is shaped and manned by their parent, which is a form of torture that no child should ever have to experience.

The Development of a Superficial Image

You can spot a narcissistic mother by how they portray themselves to people outside of your family or even outside of your relationship with her. Yes, narcissistic mothers will frequently wear several different masks even within one household, for example: Abusing their child in private and pretending nothing ever happened when the child's father is around.

The development of a superficial image that portrays your mother as someone who never does anything wrong is a strategy that she uses to protect herself from her consequences.

She does this to groom others into believing her and not her child, which means that she can defend her primary source of fulfilling her cruel and unusual needs. This way, when she openly belittles and bullies her child, the people around her believe it is warranted, and the child has no hopes of escaping the experience.

CHAPTER 6:

The Maternal Narcissistic Gaslighting

The common characteristics of victims of narcissistic abuse are low self-esteem, guilt, shame, poor self-image, despair, depression, anxiety, self-doubt, insomnia, trust issues, isolation, and even paranoia. These are evident to those who have suffered abuse from a covert narcissist. In most cases, the narcissist was someone very close to the victim, such as a parent, a sibling, or their best friend, which is why having one in your life can be so devastating. These are the people who were always supposed to have your back. Unfortunately, sometimes that is not the truth.

If everything you have read so far sounds too familiar to you, I hope it brings you relief to know that what you have experienced or are experiencing is not something you are imagining. You are not going crazy. You have been gaslighted just like every victim of narcissistic abuse is. It might be comforting to know that they chose you as a worthy supply, not because you are worthless, crazy, oversensitive, and unattractive or anything else they made you believe. You need to know that narcissists pick their victims only if the victim has something to offer, be it your optimism, intelligence, empathy, status, money, or good looks that they used to show you around. Or all of the above.

Many who are or have been in a relationship with such a damaging individual lived or lived in a state of denial because covert narcissists are manipulators of the first class and will twist the mind even of the most intelligent person. So, don't beat yourself up. You are not alone in this, and we will bust the covert together, understand who they are, but most importantly, focus on you and how you can heal from such toxic energy only a closer narcissist can bring into your life.

The Maternal Narcissistic Gaslighting

If you've ever had to deal with a narcissist, then chances are you've been a victim of a certain tactic of hers called "gaslighting." But what is gaslighting about, anyway?

In 1944, a movie was released, titled "Gaslight," adapted from a 1938 play by Patrick Hamilton, also titled "Gas Light." The film starred Ingrid Bergman, Charles Boyer, and Joseph Cotten, among others.

In the movie, Ingrid plays a woman who's the victim of her narcissistic husband. Her husband enjoys making her think she's going crazy. He manipulates things to make her believe she is losing her mind. When her husband sneaks off to the attic in search of hidden jewels, the gaslights in the house get dimmer. Ingrid's character notices the constant dimming, but her husband keeps insisting she only imagines it. I highly recommend you watch the movie if you can.

If you have ever dealt with a narcissist, or you have to deal with one right now, then you most likely have been "gaslight" more than a few times. Gaslighting is abuse. It's psychological and verbal. The narcissist employs this tactic insidiously, making you begin to wonder about your sanity. You're not sure all your marbles are there. You no longer trust your memory. You don't trust that your version of reality is the real deal and not a result of skewed thinking.

The narcissist can never be held accountable for the bad stuff they do. Heaven forbid that! It's much better to pass the blame on to someone else. It's someone else's fault and never theirs.

In passing off the blame, the narcissist will deny they were ever in the wrong. They'll accuse you of being the bad guy. They'll lead the argument or conversation somewhere far offs the mark. They'll tell outrageous lies to knock you off your center completely. You find yourself wondering if you didn't imagine the whole thing or make some sort of grave error in judgment, and it's all your fault.

A Power Play

In the end, gaslighting is a power play. It's a way of abusing you, emotionally and psychologically. The gaslighter knows how to get even more control over you. They gaslight you because they know if they've got you thinking you're nuts, then they've really got you.

It's never really a sudden thing. The process is a slow burn. If I told you the sky was pink, you'd dismiss it out of hand. But if I gradually begin to manipulate things to make the sky appear pink to you and make you think you're the only one who ever thought it was blue, you're more likely to believe me overtime because I'm wearing down your defenses, bit by bit.

The sad thing about being gas lit is the effects can last a long, long time, if not forever. Your mental health is sabotaged. You begin to mistrust everyone and everything you've ever known. Above all else, you find yourself unable to have a healthy relationship after the damage has been done.

CHAPTER 7:

How Can Someone Deal With a Narcissistic Mother?

To move on from the narcissistic abuse you faced as a child, and you need to learn how to cope with the fact your mother is a narcissist. This isn't going to happen overnight. It will take a lot of time. In fact, it will take years to fully let go of everything which caused you pain and suffering throughout your childhood. Even if you feel you are not ready to forgive your mother for everything that happened, you should still focus on the coping strategies for yourself. After all, one of the most important steps, when you begin forgiving those who harmed you, is forgiving yourself.

Understand What Narcissism Is

The best way to begin to acknowledge the personality disorder is by understanding what Narcissism is. One of the biggest challenges that someone who struggles with a personality disorder and someone who doesn't often understand the personality disorder. This goes for both people involved. If you believe you could be a narcissistic mother, it is hard to acknowledge that you could have a personality disorder.

When it comes to educating yourself about narcissistic personality disorder, you don't just want to read books and online resources. You want to watch documentaries about Narcissism, especially when it comes to narcissistic parents. You can always join support groups on social media sites, such as Facebook, and meet other people who grew up with narcissistic parents. You can also learn about Narcissism by speaking to a therapist.

Understand You Are Suffering

Not only do you need to understand narcissistic personality disorder, but you should realize that you are suffering as a consequence of it. Unfortunately, you are likely suffering from the after-effects of being raised by a narcissist more than you realize. Of course, you will be able to heal. However, you need to identify how you are suffering to overcome them.

You Are Always Blaming Yourself

Narcissistic mothers will often blame their children for anything wrong. Because of this, you might believe that everything is your fault. No matter what happens, you will find a way to blame yourself.

This is partly because he is trying to understand why his mother acts the way she does; or partly because you probably think something you said or did caused her to behave this way. So constantly blaming yourself, wondering where you went wrong, eventually leaves you with low self-esteem, making it difficult for you to motivate yourself to do it right. You might think to yourself, "If I were a better child, my mother would love me more." You might also feel if you were quieter, less visible around the house, or listened to her more often, then she would care for you more.

Post-Traumatic Stress Disorder (PTSD)

When people go through traumatic events, they can develop a psychological disorder called Post Traumatic Stress Disorder (PTSD). This typically occurs in traumatized and abused people by someone close to them, in this case, their mother. Psychologically, the symptoms of PTSD include flashbacks of the traumatic event, mistrust, severe anxiety, and fear. Behavioral signs of PTSD include hostility, self-destructive behavior, sleep disturbances, irritability, and social isolation ("Symptoms of PTSD | Anxiety and Depression Association of America, ADAA," n.d.).

Insecure Attachment

Secure attachment is when people are able to build warm, caring, and healthy relationships. Insecure attachment happens when a child is unable to learn about a healthy relationship. They might feel the only way they can secure love is by giving the person whatever they desire—a behavior that has been reinforced by their mother, who would only love them when they obeyed her every word and did exactly what she wanted.

Another way someone can show insecure attachment is through anxious attachment. This is when people will demand to be loved by the person they love. They might chase the person and become angry when they don't receive the attention they desire. This isn't a direct form of Narcissism. It is the way they learned how to love from their mother.

Avoidant attachment is another form of insecure attachment. This is when you have trouble trusting someone, and you fear what love is. You will often socially isolate yourself because of this fear. You might refuse to contact someone who has shown an interest in you, even if you like them.

You Might Be a High Achiever

Some people who grew up with narcissistic mothers will strive to do their best, to a perfectionist degree. They might do this to prove to their mother they are hardworking and talented. They might do this because it helps them feel better about themselves, hence increasing their self-esteem. We have a human need to be acknowledged and to feel that we are enough.

When we are repeatedly told we're not good enough, we will continue trying everything we can to prove we are good enough. Conversely, the other side of this scenario is giving up and not working toward any goals.

You can choose either path.

You Don't Trust Other People

One of your biggest struggles is trusting another person. It doesn't matter if you are in a close relationship with someone; you will still struggle with trusting them. This is because you couldn't trust your mother. We learn how to trust people based on our interactions with our parents. If we don't know how they will react to any situation or lied to us or didn't give us the attention we crave, we cannot trust them. Psychologically, you ask yourself if you can't trust your mother, how you can trust anyone else.

You Struggle to Understand Who You Are

Because of the control your mother held over your life, you don't understand who you are as an individual. You lack a sense of self, you might not have any goals, and you don't know what you want in your life. There are many children of narcissists who, when asked, will tell people they don't know how or why they ended up in their careers. They didn't know what they wanted, but they knew they needed a job.

It is important to understand that how narcissists suffer differs more than the ways children suffer. For example, a covert narcissist might feel guilt over their actions and some of the emotional pain they cause because they feel more strongly than other narcissists. Therefore, they feel other people's emotions, which means they can understand this when they hurt someone.

Some narcissists will struggle when they realize they have a narcissistic personality disorder. If you struggle with your psychological disorder, such as depression, anxiety, or even a learning disability, then you can imagine the emotions which arise when you discover you have a narcissistic personality disorder. You understand how it makes you feel isolated, different from everyone else, and how you can lose your sense of identity. A narcissistic mother can feel the same way. They need encouragement and support so that they can manage their psychological disorder effectively.

Accept Your Mother Won't Be Able to Receive a Cure

Another step to take toward healing is by accepting your mother will not be able to change officially. Unfortunately, Narcissism is incurable. Even if she takes the effort to go to therapy to learn strategies and how to live with a narcissistic personality disorder, she will always have this disorder.

You should never assume that your mother will take charge and talk to a therapist or try to turn her life around. If she works to do this, it's a significant step, and you should do what you can as her child to be as supportive as you can. However, you will also want to talk to a therapist to learn the best ways to support her.

The biggest reason you need to accept your mother won't change because this will keep you from false hope. No matter what happens, you will always want to feel unconditional love from your mother. However, your mother can't give you this because of Narcissism. Hence clinging on to the false hope that she can change will make you more susceptible to further mental and emotional abuse.

You also need to ensure you understand your mother's behavior is not difficult; it is merely abnormal. Your mother's behavior follows the path of "my way or the highway." She can't compromise to agree with someone else. The wires in her brain don't allow her to think this way. She puts her need to be in control above a healthy and stable relationship with you. Unfortunately, this is a part of her personality you can't change.

If you struggle with Narcissism, it can be hard to learn that you can't change your colors. This is because narcissistic personality disorder is something that you can't get rid of. However, it is something that you can learn to manage and navigate effectively, so you can go on to build healthy relationships.

CHAPTER 8:

How a Narcissistic Mother Affects Childhood

Self-Doubt

Being the narcissist's kid is that you are programmed to feel like there is something wrong with you from an early age.

You may not think that this is the case initially, but your narcissistic mother will work hard to make you believe this. And believe it, you will, because you're naturally wired to trust your parents, and you have not yet gained the ability to think about problems as a child objectively

These tender formative years are the best for the narcissistic mother to work her voodoo on your mind.

Unrealistic Expectations of Yourself

Throughout your life with your narcissistic mother, she continued to feed you with a lie, through her actions and words, covertly and overtly. What was the lie? That you could earn her love if you did your very best. So, you grew up thinking you just had to be smart enough, or pretty enough, or strong enough, or whatever-enough, and you would have the love, approval, and attention that your mother has been withholding from you. She made you believe that you had to strive to be a perfect child, and once you were perfect, then she could love you.

Crushed Self-Esteem

Narcissistic mothers teach their children that they are worth nothing, right from birth. All your wants and needs mean nothing to the narc, which naturally leads you to wonder why you're not getting them met. It must be because you're not worth it, you conclude.

The narcissistic mother finds so many different tactics to get you to believe you are nothing at all. Sadly, it worked. Even as an adult, you deal with feelings of inadequacy and low self-esteem. You do matter, though. You always have. That voice in mind says you don't mean anything. That's one more lie embedded in your noggin by your mother. That's one more lie you don't need to hold on to any longer.

Zero Confidence

The fact is this is something that plagues every child who had a narcissistic parent raising them. You find you're not so confident, no matter where you find yourself. Even when you're alone, you're somehow judging yourself. Since you're always used to being judged by your mother, you do the same to yourself and expect others. Also, since she's spent so much time and energy cutting you down, it's no wonder that you don't feel so sure about yourself or your skills.

Lack of Trust

As the child of a narcissistic mother, you find it incredibly hard to trust others. Not just any others, though. Women. In my case, it was any woman old enough to be my mother. It's like you expect every other woman to be just like your mother—unpredictable, manipulative, full of rage, toxic. Growing up with a narc for a mom means you always had to be on your toes. It could then lead you to project your mother's traits onto others. You find yourself unable and unwilling to trust them. It also doesn't help that you keep finding yourself with narcissists for friends and lovers. The inclination is to keep your heart shut for good.

Concealing Emotions

As a kid, you learned that you should not express your emotions. You are not allowed to be mad; you are not permitted to be hurt. You'd better not show that you're either of these things while your narcissistic mother abuses you. Did you scrape your elbow? Is it bleeding terribly? Too bad. You would better not shout. Then you should better not cry. You'd better not pout. Your narcissistic mother is evil and selfish. The last thing she needs is you bothering her with your wailing. Unless, of course, there is some drama in it for her, meaning she has an audience and a chance to shine at being Super Mom.

You were also not allowed to express your positive emotions. If you did, she would feel like you were a threat, and she would do something about it. She also resents it when you're pleased. She resents when someone or something other than her is the reason for your smile. So, she sets out to make you miserable in; anyway she can. Did you just get a toy from an uncle? She'll cease it once he's gone and only ever give it to you once he's around. It happened to me. True story. Did you get an A in Math, but the A was 99 percent, not 100? Then she will dismiss you. Again, true story.

Disjointed Thoughts and Emotions

It is difficult for you to know your true feelings about the circumstances in your life. You don't even know what your thoughts are about a given situation. You're so used to believing that you cannot trust your point of view.

You're so used to looking to your narcissistic mother to tell you what to think and how to feel. Where others can spontaneously express their thoughts and feelings, you need a lot of time to check and understand.

When someone says something rude or horrible to you, you do not realize it at the moment. It hits you much, much sooner than they really should not have said what they said or treated you the way they did. It's almost as if the wires connecting your emotions to your mind have been chewed up and disconnected. But you can train yourself to combine both. In the process of healing, you will work this out.

What you'll find is that you'll get better and better at expressing yourself at the moment as the days go by.

Unwillingness to Stake Your Claim

Growing up with your narcissistic mother means you were all about fulfilling her needs. You learned very quickly to ignore your own needs because if you didn't, you'd get into trouble for it. You were programmed to believe that getting your own needs met was incredibly selfish, and you ought to be ashamed of that.

Something to consider now you're an adult is what true selfishness is. When you're selfish, you make things that are not about you to revolve around you. There are, however, times when something is actually about you. There's nothing wrong with that! In reality, your graduation is about you. Your birthday is about you. Your promotion at work is about you. Your newly born is about you and the baby, and that's that. You are not selfish for drawing a line and staking your claim on what is about you.

Overachieving and Underachieving

With the children of narcissistic mothers, it usually pans out one of two ways. It's either the child decides to do all they can to prove themselves and finally feel good enough. So, they become overachievers, or they are continually sabotaging themselves, frequently having problems with finances, and always failing because deep down, they do not feel deserving of good things.

It is because you were taught as a child that you're not good enough, smart enough, fast enough, pretty enough, and so on. You're not enough of those things for you to deserve approval, love, attention, validation, or empathy.

You may have received money or other material things, but more often than not, it was envied to you after you had to grovel and beg. So, you grow up as an adult who has a problem with accepting the good life has to offer.

Constantly Feeling Lonely

If you have somehow managed to keep in touch with your family as an adult, you somehow still feel lonely with them around. You've been unable to connect fully with them, no matter how hard you try.

Why this happens is that they have no idea who the real you are. You can't even show them your authentic self because to do so would be to make yourself vulnerable. After all, the mother says that the real you are undesirable.

You might also find it incredibly difficult to establish connections with people outside of your family. Lack of trust, or the anxiety you feel about whether you're worth knowing, or the lack of social skills because your mother kept you isolated.

Social Anxiety

You most likely have to deal with crippling social anxiety. You don't know what's right and what isn't. You don't know the best way to behave when you're with others. You wonder if you're too quiet or too loud. You wonder if you were meant to go with red in place of blue. Where no one else can see, you carry a heavy load of shame deep down. You're ashamed of yourself. You're ashamed of who you are. You are worried that nobody is going to love you. As a result, you find yourself creating a reality in which no one loves you, and that becomes a self-fulfilling prophecy. It's not because you're not the right person or you're not sweet. It's because somehow others can tune into what we think of ourselves on a subconscious level, and they reflect you what you think.

Never Simply Accepting Compliments

It is an unbelievably common effect of being raised by a narcissistic mother. Usually, it's because she never the few times complimented you, it was followed by something to cut you down. When another person approves you, she would be quick with a cutting remark.

Since you don't believe you need to be complimented, you always throw them a compliment of your own. Now, this is tricky. There are times when it's excellent to give praise back, and times it isn't. How can you say the difference between both of them? Well, ask yourself why you're complimenting them. Are you doing so because you genuinely mean it, or are you doing so because you feel obligated to pay them back? There's your answer.

Depression

Children of narcissistic parents are often prone to depression. It's sad but true that there is no surprise that this happens. You would not be authorized to be your true self. You don't even know who your true self is. You feel like you don't fit in anywhere. You want to interact with others, but you're frightened, don't know how, or can't trust. Your self-esteem is almost nonexistent, thanks to my dear old mom. You don't have the skills you need to move forward in life. You're always being criticized by your mother, despite your best efforts and intentions.

Even when you're not with her, her voice keeps on going in your head, telling you how you're worthless, and you've got problems that can't be solved, telling you you're a horrible human being in general. You've believed all of that for years. You've watched other kids with well-adjusted parents and wondered why things were not that way for you. You've sacrificed all that you can to just get even a little bit of love or attention from your mother.

CHAPTER 9:

How a Narcissistic Mother Affects Adolescence

I f a narcissist raised you, it would affect how you are acting now directly. Some individuals might even grow fearful that they have become narcissists themselves. Though this is possible, you have to remember that we will usually have this lifestyle's side effects rather than the actual toxic thoughts that a narcissist usually has.

The Ways Manipulation Has Occurred

As we grew up, many children of narcissistic moms dealt with constant criticism, judgment, and harsh feedback on every little thing you did. It was like you were at fault for not doing it, but then when you did do it, someone was there to give you negative feedback right away. There were often many situations in which neither person could win in the end.

It was a form of manipulation. It occurred throughout small instances, but after months and months of negativity spewing from the narcissistic parent's mouth, it became the way that their children thought. These manipulation tactics gave the narcissist the upper hand. When there was a confrontation, even when the narcissist might have been blatantly wrong, the abused would still consider themselves at fault because the abuser had manipulated them. They struggle to understand their thoughts and constantly judge themselves because of what the narcissistic mom might have said to them initially.

How A Narcissist Influences Your Mindset?

All of the manipulation tactics will get into your head. It is almost like you become brainwashed. Not all cases are as hard as the brainwashing methods that we know to be true; however, you will often still hear the voice of your narcissistic mother in the back of your head. Perhaps you are picking out clothing, getting a haircut, or decorating your home. You might end up hearing their judgments in the background. Maybe something terrible happened, and you feel bad about yourself. Perhaps you still hear your mother's voice judging you and affirming that you did something wrong. It is very normal to hear your abuser's voice in your head, even in moments where you want them to go away.

When you start to have feelings surface, you might try to stuff them right back down. A narcissist doesn't like talking about anyone's feelings other than their own. It becomes normalized to ignore any emotion that you have. Rather than looking at your feelings, you might end up taking on the feelings of others. If there is a situation where multiple people are upset, rather than taking care of yourself, you might try to play caretaker for everyone else.

The Emotional Roller Coaster Created

Living with a narcissist means going on an emotional roller coaster. There are ups and downs, and no matter what you try to do, you will always be strapped in along for the ride, unable to break out of this toxic cycle. A narcissistic roller coaster starts with that good feeling first.

You're excited about what's going to happen. You are building a healthy relationship, and they seem to be love bombing you. This phase is more apparent in romantic relationships that have just started. For example, let's say that there is a couple: a boyfriend and a girlfriend; the narcissist is the boy. He has chosen a girl to pursue because she's sweet, caring, and emotional. They hit it off, and they start the love-bombing phase. He tells her everything that she wants to hear.

It is more complicated in a parent-child relationship because you're with them from the moment you're born. You don't have that initial meeting period where you get to know them. You don't have the chance to escape before it's too late.

Even if red flags are there, you won't be able to spot them, especially as someone who's four, seven, twelve, etc. This love-bombing period likely comes during a different life event. Maybe they got a new job. Perhaps they finally quit drinking. A new house, marriage, and other life events could be the start of this roller coaster, where you feel like things are good, and everything is going to be happy as it should be.

You might end up constantly criticizing yourself, thinking that you should have done better in other areas that you have control over. It's easier to label things as either positive or negative because that's the only control you've ever had.

Your ability to reason can be skewed as you grow because you weren't given a chance to develop fully. It means that you'll end up not having a clear perspective down the line, so labeling things is the way you reason.

It creates an "all-or-nothing" kind of mindset. It will make you doubt yourself, and you might even get to the point where you hurt yourself. Your relationships can become damaged, and you might experience frequent anxiety. It can take all stems simply because you don't know how to not blame yourself for the things that your narcissistic parents might have done to you.

Unrealistic Self-Appraisal

The issue with this is that we either think that we are terrible people or better than everyone else. Did you get a good grade on your test? You must be smarter than the rest of your classmates. Did you fail? You're the dumbest person ever to walk the planet. This switch between our perspectives is not healthy. It's just one test, not the defining moment of your life. Did you make a cake that everyone enjoyed? You're a talented chef. Did you drop that cake? You ruined the party and the rest of the year as well. It is so not the case! We can't allow ourselves to think in such extreme ways because it is like a teetering seesaw bound to shoot us like a cannon into the air when one side drops. If you keep yourself in such high esteem, you will feel even worse when something terrible happens.

You deserve to feel good about yourself! You should be proud of your accomplishments! We have to ensure that we are holding ourselves at the same level that we hold other people. If someone else did the common thing, would you similarly judge them that you do yourself? It is what we'll have to ask ourselves in the process of healing continually.

Poor Self-Discipline

Because we weren't able to regulate our emotions as children, this will directly affect our self-discipline. Self-discipline doesn't mean that you're hard on yourself and always criticizing your actions. Those who have a high level of discipline know what they need to get done, know what they want in the end, and have a great action plan for getting those things.

The reason that you struggle with this isn't that you don't have the discipline needed to get what you want. You are not able to control your own emotions. You're struggling to recognize and regulate your feelings; therefore, you will continue to act impulsively. The problem isn't with you and your personality. You were never given proper lessons on controlling your feelings and working through them when you need to.

Anger Towards Yourself

You often can't take the anger out on the other person, so it's easier to take it out on yourself. If you did ever express your emotions in the past, you might have had to keep them bottled up after that because you were punished for saying something. We're frequently taught that violence is bad as well. If you can't express your feelings to other people, then the only thing that we think we have the option to do in the end is to take that anger out on ourselves.

What happens is that this anger doesn't go away. Imagine shaking up a bottle of soda. If you shake it too hard, it can end up exploding. If you shake it just hard enough, throughout time, it won't explode. However, once you finally do open it up, it will be a lot different from what it was in the first place. If you take this anger and do nothing with it, you can end up letting it become something that destroys you.

Finally, anger might make you take things out on yourself. You might self-medicate through alcohol, cut different parts of your body, or deprive yourself of things that you need, like food, or even just having fun in general. When you are angry, you can turn that inwards and self-harm because it makes you feel in control. You are the one in charge of punishing yourself. When you have experienced pain so frequently from other people, it makes you feel good to inflict pain on yourself. Finally, you are in control instead of others who have had power in the past. Simultaneously, self-harm can also make us feel as though we have a responsibility and take care of ourselves. Perhaps you binge but purge through laxatives or vomiting later. You are inflicting the pain yourself, and then you are taking care of it yourself, which can make us feel very accomplished with higher self-esteem. If you don't manage your anger, it means not managing this part of your emotions.

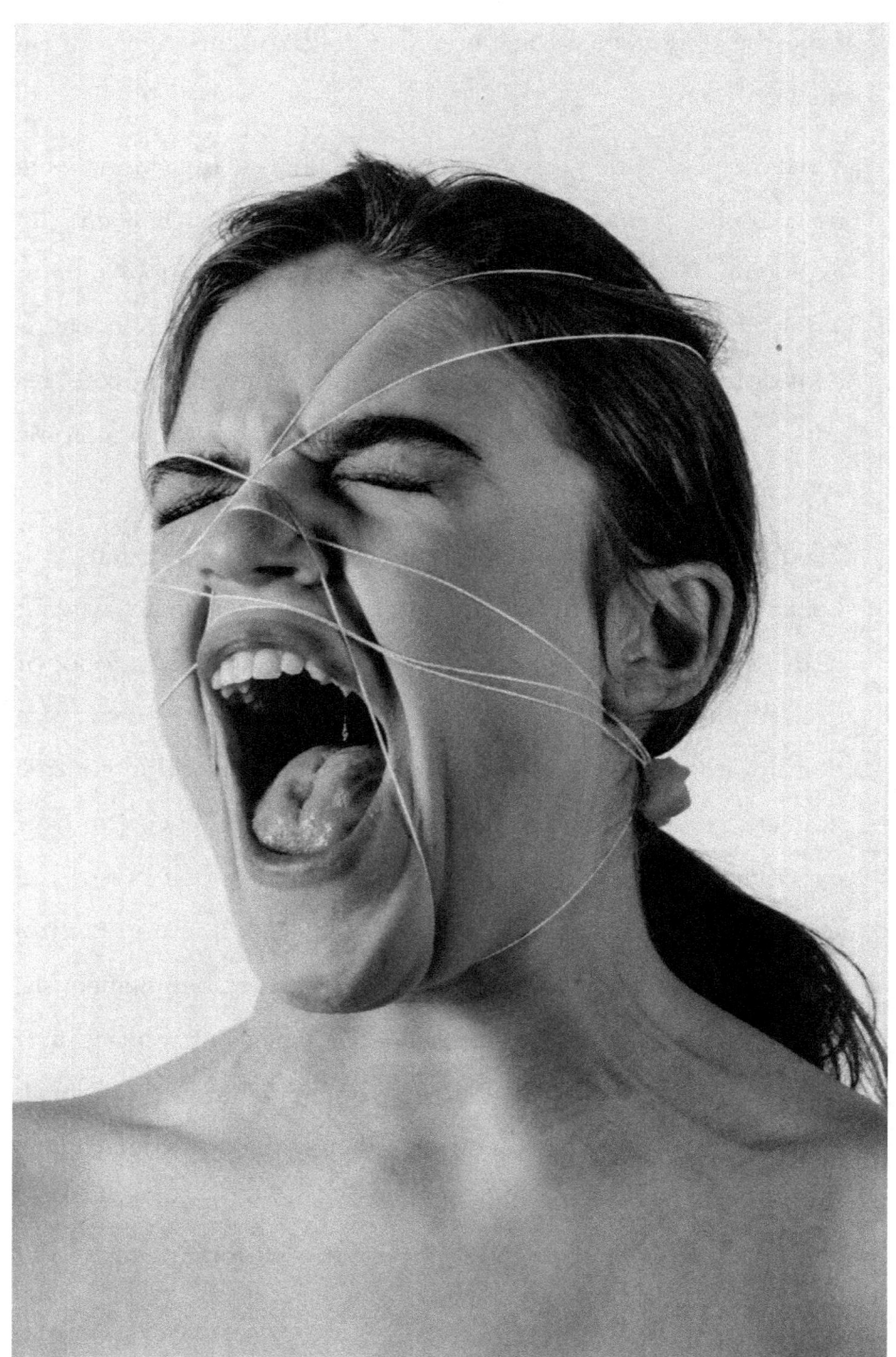

CHAPTER 10:

Narcissist Mother and Her Sons

A man's relationship with his mother is as complicated just as a relationship with a daughter and her mother.

A first specific area of the relationship between the male child and the narcissistic mother is her behavior with all people who have a relationship with his son.

Another big trouble is the relationship with her husband and the father of her son. Often a narcissistic mom has married a very co-dependent man. She puts him down in front of the children and makes fun of him sexually. Lots of men have witnessed how their narcissistic mothers have battered their fathers in front of them, maybe not in front of neighbors and other family members but behind closed doors.

Your father, whom your mom is putting down, and you don't realize that what she's doing is really conditioning you to be afraid, to be like him.

She's trying to make sure that you feel dependent upon her and obligated to her, and you have the feeling of disappointment. She's trying to find a way to make sure that you don't do what her dad did to her, which is to abandon her. That's the way she sees it.

Mom needs to know that her son has put her in the center of his life. Therefore, the son of a narcissistic mother is terrified, living in a state of survival. There's also the loss of the self, and this is a problem in terms of emotional development.

The young boy is not permitted to feel free enough to explore his environment without fear. So there's a lot of insecurity in the young boy who has a narcissistic mom, which carries over to adolescence when this young man wants to bring home a date.

The mom will find a problem with the date and will actually gaslight the date, creating many problems. The son will get the message that the mom is not happy that he brought the girl home. Statements like "That girl only wants you for your money," "That girl's going to go out and get pregnant by you," or "You're going to have to support her and some kid for the rest of your life" will be floated around. You could be 12, and that's the kind of crap that your mother will be telling you, so you're getting the message.

It also happens that the narcissistic mothers would always play sick the minute her son wants to go out to play baseball or tell her he has a girlfriend. Mommy would get sick, and the boy would have to abandon and prove to his mother that she is number one in his life, and this gets repeated over and over.

Narcissistic mom will see the women in your life as competitors. Your wife will feel like there's a mistress in the room, and even though you are not sleeping with your mom, this energy will be a part of your life.

And because she has primed you to fear being able to set a boundary, you, as the son of a narcissistic mom, may have marital problems or relationship problems with females who are feeling this heat from mom.

This tug-of-war in the mind of the son of the narcissistic mothers could be serious. They love their mother, who has conditioned them to be afraid too much to let them go. Also, they struggle with addiction or low self-esteem, or that situation where you feel like an alien in your own skin.

If you are the son of a narcissistic mother, you may have tremendous cognitive dissonance. You might love and hate her at the same time. You might have immense rage when it comes to women because you're so angry at your mom, but you might not understand where it's coming from…and that rage is valid. This doesn't mean you abuse women or blame your girlfriend or daughter or the cashier you know at the corner store.

It means that as the son of a narcissistic mother, you recognize that you have been abused. It means that you recognize that you have not been permitted to grow, develop, and attune yourself to what is right. You have not been permitted to be who you are. You have had your emotions screwed with.

You have been manipulated and toyed with for this woman's agenda, and the anger and the rage that you feel is valid, and that's why it's important to work this out.

It's not your fault if you've experienced co-dependency. Lots of men who have narcissistic mothers find themselves co-dependent. They tend to be the type of men that women walk all over, are afraid of making women angry, attract women who lie and take advantage of them.

There is also another take on this: Some of these men end up with high narcissistic traits themselves. Where in some situations, mom has put her son on a pedestal, and mom seems very sweet and very coddling and very nurturing and all of that, but there's almost an emotional incest that can happen, and mom isn't as overt as another narcissistic mom. She's kind of passive-aggressive in her comments about women. She's passive-aggressive about being left alone, but the message is, "don't ever leave me; I have to come first." So, she might say things like "that girl's not good enough for you" or "she should treat you better."

But then, what happens could be like a mother-son tag-team. If you're not aware of the enmeshment and the dependency upon mom's approval and need for validation and the way she's manipulating the situation, you make sure that she's the goddess of your life forever.

If you are the son of a narcissistic mother, there are so many ways this can play out. If you have an overt narcissistic mother, it might be easier for you to see it, and you might be able to recognize that your mother turned you against every woman you ever brought into the house. She talked negatively about everybody: every man, every woman, and every child.

As you grow up and attract females, you will have to find something wrong with every female. If you get married, your mom will be a constant source of pain for you and your wife; she will resent your children, she will resent your wife, and she will resent you.

When you tell her that something remarkable happened, she'll find a way to downgrade it. She plans to get you to worry about her. If you give her any idea that she is being replaced, there's going to be an issue. It is important if you're the son of a narcissistic mother, you may feel very conflicted and may have anger and rage if you are not aware of what's going on.

Some men take on narcissistic traits, so they feel conflict with their mother. They felt controlled by their mothers, so their plan is no woman's going to control me, no girlfriend or wife will control me because they're a little bit more aware of how they feel about their mother. They might even hate their mother.

They still might want a relationship with a woman and a sexual relationship even, but they might struggle with conflict because their mother was such a tyrant. There are so many ways this programming can manifest in your life.

You must understand what has happened to you as a result, and you must understand the tremendous consequences of having a narcissistic mother.

You have been told that life is scary when it comes to getting married; there's always a chance that you could get divorced, and there's still a chance that a woman could abandon you.

There is always a chance for abandonment issues to manifest. That's something we need to heal from, especially if we have narcissistic mothers, because that fear might cause us to be emotionally avoidant and unavailable. It might cause us to be highly narcissistic because we're afraid of being abandoned.

It's so crucial that all of us recognize how having narcissistic parents affect us as adults, and we have to heal this gaping wound inside of our hearts that have been created by this narcissistic parent.

We have a need to be vulnerable, but we're frightened; we're afraid of being engulfed and enmeshed with. We need to trust people, but we don't trust people. We need to be loved, but we don't love ourselves.

This is what happens as adults, and so if you are the son of a narcissistic mother, there is help. The most important thing you can do is research and understand the consequences of what has happened to you.

Understand that if you've had a dad who has been beaten down by a narcissistic mother and hasn't seen a man assert boundaries and as a result, you don't know how to reserve boundaries with a female or with other people, it is not your fault.

You might need to talk to specialists and psychotherapists that are skilled in the area of narcissistic abuse and childhood trauma, and those that you feel can attune themselves to you. You have to think about all of that before you go into therapy.

It's very important that if you're going to deal with the psychotherapist, you deal with somebody who, when you interview them, you feel like they can attune themselves to you. What's happened to you is that you have had your feelings completely invalidated and have been marginalized.

Conclusion

Thank you for reading this book. I hope it was able to provide you with all the required information you need to deal with a narcissistic mother.

We all have parents, and we expect our parents to be good to us, take care of us and protect us. But we need to know that everyone is different; there are times when the parent that God has given us is a narcissist. It becomes worse when this is our mother we are talking about.

It is your sole responsibility to internalize and practice for ultimate results. You may need to break down important points and prioritize them for easy and coordinated steps to action.

Mothers are supposed to be protective and loving. They need to nurture us and make us grow into responsible human beings. But when they abuse us, things change, and they change for the worst.

A narcissist is a person that suffers from a disorder. When you have a parent who is a narcissist, you have no option but to go through the ordeal because you have to live with them.

There are millions of people who struggle with a narcissistic personality disorder, and most of them are able to manage their personality disorder as well as possible. If you are a child who grew up with a narcissistic mother, you also understand that you are not alone. In fact, you face some of the same challenges, such as trusting other people that most other children of narcissists do.